Published Worldwide by
The Rusty Publishing Company
1st Printing

Special Thanks to Julie Austin

The Unicorn Has One Horn

By Rusty Austin
Illustrated by Frank Henderson

For Carlo

TABLE OF ANIMALS

Unicorn ...

Hedgehog ...

Moose ...

Housecat ...

Black Footed Ferret ...

Tomcat ...

Rattlesnake ...

Barking Seal ...

Cougar ...

Wolf ...

Raccoon ...

Tapir ...

Bengal Tiger ...

Crane ...

Leopard ...

Blind Fruit Bat ...

Badger ...

Horse ...

Squirrel ...

Wombat ...

Lioness ...

Blue Whale ...

Panther ...

Myna Bird ...

Elephant Seal ...

Porpoise ...

Polar Bear ...

Crocodile ...

Great White Shark ...

White Tailed Deer ...

Iguana ...

Bobcat ...

Lazy Opossum ...

Brown Field Mouse ...

Sly Red Fox ...

Elk ...

Gopher ...

DO IT YOURSELF

Garter Snake ...

Chickadee ...

The Unicorn has one horn
they say she can fly
but I've never seen one
up in the sky

The Moose is large
with a mighty rack

if you see one coming
stay back!

The Housecat
has very soft fur
when you pet her
she likes to purr

The Black Footed Ferret
is an agile fellow
but on Sunday afternoon
he's slow and mellow

The Rattlesnake rattles
when she's about
which is the best way
for you to find out

The Barking Seal barks
when she feels happy
and flaps her flippers
when she feels flappy

The Cougar roams
far and wide
pay attention
she likes to hide

The Wolf will always
run in a pack
that way each one always
has the other one's back

In the afternoon
you won't see The Raccoon
she doesn't like daylight
and only comes out at night

The Tapir has
a stubby snout
he uses it to
sniff food out

The Bengal Tiger is strong
her claws are long
if you see one, run!

The Crane has long legs a
long neck
and beak

so she can
stand in the water
and pluck fish
from the creek

The Leopard has lots
of fine looking dots
on her fur coat
that you may call spots

The Blind Fruit Bat
can't see at night
so he uses his ears
to guide his flight

The Badger has claws
that are sharp and wide
in a digging contest
you'll want him on your side

The Horse likes to run
around the track
and he runs so fast
he's already back

The Squirrel gathers nuts
all day every day
because he knows
winter is on its way

The Wombat
is short and stout
he will be your friend
no doubt

The Lioness hunts all night
and sleeps all day
but she always stands guard
when her cubs come out to play

The Blue Whale has to eat
krill by the ton

to get enough energy
so she can have fun

The Panther has eyes
that are big and bright
and his fur is black
so he can hunt at night

The Myna Bird
likes to speak

but don't get her started
or she'll talk for a week

The Elephant Seal is large
and easily pleased
but don't get in his way
or you'll likely get squeezed

The Porpoise loves
to swim in the sea

she jumps with joy
so fast and free

The Polar Bear lives
on the Arctic Ice
stay far away
is my advice

The Crocodile has
a toothy smile
watch out for him
if you go for a swim

The Great White Shark
swims and eats

with his great white fins
and his great white teeths

The White Tailed Deer
is not easily seen
but more from behind
if you know what I mean

The Iguana is brown
and green and gold

his tail is long
and his skin is cold

The Bobcat hides
way up in the trees

you see him, then not
just like the breeze

The Lazy Opossum
hangs from a tree

where she uses her tail
to swing high and free

The Brown Field Mouse
is so very small
he comes and goes
and isn't seen at all

The Elk will bugle
his intentions loudly

his antlers are enormous
and he wears them proudly

The Gopher digs tunnels
here and there
she'll dig for miles
to anywhere

THE END

ABOUT THE AUTHOR

Rusty Austin began his career writing book and movie reviews at his community college newspaper, The Rapp Street Journal, where he eventually became editor in chief. He moved on to graduate from UCLA Film School and then to Hollywood where he worked for many years as a TV producer. Along the way he discovered a talent for writing poetry. As his Hollywood career wound down he wrote a series of Facebook posts which gradually morphed into a large number of kid friendly and adult savvy poems. He has always had a soft spot for animals and food, so that's what he writes poems about! At the urging of his Facebook family, he turned those posts into books. His books always include a short DIY section to encourage kids to write their own poems and draw their own animals or favorite foods.

Also by Rusty
The Two-Headed Snake
The Unicorn Has One Horn
Beware the Grizzly Bear
The Carrot Is Orange